RIPLEY's SPACE

Believe It or Not!®

KT-479-434

RIPLEY

C333537427

Written by Dr. Mike Goldsmith
Consultant Clint Twist

PUBLISHING

Publisher Anne Marshall

Editorial Director Rebecca Miles

Picture Researcher James Proud

Editors Lisa Regan, Rosie Alexander, Charlotte Howell

Proofreader Judy Barratt

Indexer Hilary Bird

Art Director Sam South

Design Rocket Design (East Anglia) Ltd

Reprographics Juice Creative Ltd

www.ripleys.com

Copyright ©2009 by Ripley Entertainment Inc.

First published in Great Britain in 2009 by Random House Books, Random House, 20 Vauxhall Bridge Road, London SW1V 2SA
www.randomhouse.co.uk

This edition 2013

Addresses for companies within The Random House Group Limited can be found at: www.randomhouse.co.uk/offices.htm

The Random House Group Limited Reg. No. 954009

All rights reserved. Ripley's, Believe It or Not! and Ripley's Believe It or Not! are registered trademarks of Ripley Entertainment Inc.

ISBN 9780099568155

10 9 8 7 6 5 4 3 2 1

No part of this publication may be reproduced in whole or in part, or stored in a retrieval system, or transmitted in any form or by any means, electronic, mechanical, photocopying, recording, or otherwise, without written permission from the publisher. For information regarding permission, write to VP Intellectual Property, Ripley Entertainment Inc., Suite 188, 7576 Kingspointe Parkway, Orlando, Florida 32819

e-mail: publishing@ripleys.com

A CIP catalogue record for this book is available from the British Library

Printed in China

PUBLISHER'S NOTE
While every effort has been made to verify the accuracy of the entries in this book, the Publishers cannot be held responsible for any errors contained in the work. They would be glad to receive any information from readers.

WARNING
Some of the stunts and activities in this book are undertaken by experts and should not be attempted by anyone without adequate training and supervision.

Contents

PAGE 24

PAGE 22

PAGE 44

Universally Speaking

Space is fascinating, and huge, and complicated. It's full of things you can see, like stars, and satellites, and the Sun. It's even more full of things you can't see, like black holes and wormholes and dark energy. Scientists have spent lifetimes trying to make sense of what's out there. How big is the Universe? How did it all begin? Where will it all end?

*Found a new word?
We will explain it
for you.*

24

WHAT'S INSIDE YOUR BOOK?

This book shows you some of space's best bits: shuttles and space stations, planets and probes, meteorites and moons, asteroids and astronauts. Every page is packed with out-of-this world info, with special Ripley's fascinating facts and amazing 'Believe It or Not!' stories. Are you ready to read on? 5-4-3-2-1...

TWISTS

It's not enough for some astronauts to go into space in a spaceship – they want to take a walk while they're there! A special protective suit (see page 40) allows EVA (extra-vehicular activity). The longest EVA was done in 2001 by two astronauts who stayed outside the International Space Station (see page 42) for nearly 9 hours.

Danger Zone
○ ASTEROIDS AND COMETS

Comets are like giant dirty snowballs. Usually comets are pretty happy orbiting far out at the edge of the Solar System, about seven trillion kilometres from Earth, but sometimes they swoop in towards the Sun, growing tails of gas and dust as they warm up.

If you've ever seen a comet, you probably weren't afraid – after all, it was just a whitish streak in the sky. Don't be fooled, though: comets can kill. In fact, it was probably a comet (or perhaps an asteroid) that wiped out the mighty dinosaurs 65 million years ago. It crashed into the Earth and the dust it threw up froze the planet, which killed the dinosaurs. And it could happen again – to us.

amazing!!

This colossal crater, seen here from space, in Australia's Northern Territory is called Gosses Bluff and is about 4.5 km wide. It was made by an asteroid or comet about 1 km across that crashed into Earth around 142 million years ago.

ASTEROID

SAY WHAT?

A small rocky body in orbit around the Sun. Many asteroids are located between the orbits of Mars and Jupiter. These are the building blocks of a planet that failed to form there.

In 2000, Comet Hyakutake had a tail 550 million km long – nearly four times longer than the distance from the Earth to the Sun!

Comets are made of ice, dust and rocky material that came from the Solar System when it was first created about 4.5 billion years ago.

oosh...

The centre of a comet is called its nucleus.

Learn fab fast facts to go with the cool pictures.

Ripley's Believe It or Not!®

Who'd have thought it? Read all about some totally out there (but totally true) stories – like the teddies sent into space. Members of Cambridge University space-flight club launched four teds on a weather balloon. The teddies wore suits made of foil, foam, plastic bottles and tape, which had been designed by schoolchildren to protect their furry friends from the -58°F temperatures.

twist it!

A comet or asteroid the size of a city crashed into Mexico's Yucatan Peninsula 65 million years ago.

A comet called Shoemaker-Levy 9 crashed into Jupiter in 1994. It hit the planet on the side that was facing away from Earth, so the impact itself wasn't seen, but huge marks could be seen in Jupiter's atmosphere for several months afterwards.

Halley is a comet that reappears every 75.3 years. There are records of its visits that go back to 25 May, 240BC.

If you had been around in 1910, when the Earth passed through the tail of a comet, you could have tried some of the anti-comet pills that were on sale. But they wouldn't have done you any good!

In 1908, a strange explosion flattened 2,150 sq km of forest in Siberia. It was probably caused by a comet exploding in the air.

WATCH IT!

25

Do the twist

This book is packed with superb sights from the known Universe. It will teach you amazing things about space, but like all Twists books, it shines a spotlight on things that are unbelievable but true. Turn the pages and find out more...

Twists are all about Believe It or Not: amazing facts, feats, and things that will make you go 'Wow!'.

Don't forget to look out for the 'twist it!' column on some pages. Twist the book to find out more fast facts about the Universe we live in.

HOW BiG?

⊙ THE UNIVERSE

Everything that exists is part of the Universe, and that's a big, big, big place. HUGE! In fact, the distance across the Universe is at least a whopping 900 billion trillion kilometres. Many scientists think that it's larger than this: it may even go on for ever!

The Universe contains at least a billion trillion stars, yet it is mostly empty space. All the stars and planets and other things we can see only make up about 5% of the Universe – the rest is called 'dark energy' and 'dark matter' – and no one knows what they are!

These smudges of light are groups of millions of stars, billions of trillions of kilometres away. The time taken for their light to cross the Universe means this picture is a few billion years out of date!

If you travelled through the Universe in a spaceship, you would never reach an edge, no matter how fast or far or long you travelled!

The Universe is expanding (getting bigger) every second.

The Universe has no centre.

How big?

JUST HOW BIG IS 900 BILLION TRILLION KILOMETRES? EVEN ON THE PAGE IT'S AN ENORMOUS NUMBER:

900,000,000,000,000,000,000,000!

seeing stars

Fancy waking up and seeing the stars above you? You don't need to sleep outdoors – artist Rip Read can paint a StarMural on your ceiling. The painting is only visible in the dark, so the 'Startist' has to work at night, with the lights out!

OUT OF THIS WORLD

It is possible that before our Universe existed there was another one, and another one before that, and another one before that...

On average, the Universe contains only one atom in every four cubic metres. This is like one lump of sugar in a box with sides 10,000 km long.

Even on the clearest, darkest night you can see fewer than 1/100,000,000,000,000,000 (one-one hundred thousand trillionth) of the stars in the Universe.

Three-quarters of the known Universe (that is, other than dark matter and dark energy) is hydrogen.

The temperature of most of the Universe is −270°C, much colder than the coldest freezer on Earth, and only 3 degrees warmer than the coldest possible temperature.

Ripley's Believe It or Not!®

UP, UP AND AWAY

SpaceShipOne was the first private manned spacecraft in space (exceeding an altitude of 100,000 m). In 2004, it was successfully launched twice within a two-week period, claiming the Ansari X prize of $10 million. The competition's aim was to boost civilian-led (rather than military-led) spaceflight. The team have joined forces with Virgin Galactic, intending to send customers into space on short trips.

SAY WHAT?

BILLION AND TRILLION

A billion is one thousand million, or 1,000,000,000. A trillion is even bigger: one million million, or 1,000,000,000,000. A billion trillion has 21 zeros on the end!

May the Force be with You

🌀 GRAVITY

Gravity, the force that holds you to the ground, also stops the Earth falling apart, keeps the Moon going around the Earth, and the Earth going around the Sun.

The more massive the planet you stand on, the stronger gravity becomes, and the more you weigh. If you could stand on Jupiter you would weigh more than twice as much as on Earth, and on the Sun you would weigh a thundering 2 tonnes. On the Moon you would weigh so little that you would be a super-Olympian, jumping about four times higher than on Earth. In deep space, far from any star or planet, you would weigh zilch, zero, nothing at all.

floaters!

🌀 **Everything** in the Universe pulls on everything else with the pull of gravity – even you and this book are strangely attracted to each other!

🌀 **Near a black hole** (see page 30) the gravity is strong enough to tear you apart.

When you are falling, you don't feel the pull of gravity – which is why astronauts in orbit are weightless, even though the Earth's gravity is nearly as strong in orbit as on the surface of the Earth. The astronauts are in a constant state of falling – but so is their spacecraft, so the astronauts float around inside.

>> space surgery >>

In 2006, surgeons from Bordeaux University carried out an operation under weightless conditions, to practise for surgery in space.

FORCEFUL STUFF

If you could survive the heat in the centre of the Earth, you would find that you weighed nothing there and could float around, because the gravity would pull you equally in all directions.

Time slows down where gravity is strong. So, if your parents spent a few decades near a black hole, they could be younger than you when they came home. This also means that people who live on mountains age faster than those living at sea level.

Neurolab was a 1998 space shuttle experiment to test the reactions of living creatures to weightless conditions. It contained 1,500 crickets, 230 swordtail fish, 130 water snails, 150 rats and 18 pregnant mice.

The gravity on some asteroids (see page 24) is so low you could jump off them.

You weigh more at the Poles and less at the Equator, due partly to the Earth's shape and partly to its spin.

twist it!

Albert Einstein discovered that gravity is a warp (bend) in time and space. Einstein was one of the world's most famous scientists. He lived from 1879 to 1955 and developed the Theory of General Relativity, about how gravity works.

Ripley's Believe It or Not!®

SAY WHAT?

ORBIT
The path of one object around another in space.

Paralympian Wojtek Czyz set a new long jump record in 2008, wearing a prosthetic leg made of space materials! The same material was used in his leg and in a spectrometer to b90e mounted on the ISS (International Space Station), as both items need to be extremely strong and light.

SAY HI to a robot Einstein! This US robot can act like a human in certain ways, such as having a conversation, recognizing faces, changing facial expressions and mimicking emotions.

FASCINATING FACT

Vesta (asteroid) 62.2 metres

JUMP AROUND >>

Want to break the world high jump record? All you have to do is go to the Moon: our space-neighbour is much less massive than the Earth, which means the pull of gravity there is less, and so is your weight, so you could jump much higher than at home. To really impress the spectators, try jumping on an asteroid like Vesta. Don't forget to take some air with you.

Pluto 24.1 metres ▶

Moon 9.2 metres ▶

Mars 4.5 metres ▶
Earth 2.4 metres ▶

Home Truths

As far as we know, Earth is the only place in the Universe where life exists. Though we live all over the place, some of our planet isn't too friendly: 71% is covered in water, and 97% of that water is too salty to drink. Temperatures at the Poles fall as low as –89°C, and in deserts they can rise to a blistering 58°C.

That's just on the surface. Inside the Earth, it gets hotter as you go deeper. It reaches about 6000°C in the core – about as hot as the surface of the Sun. In the other direction, up in the air, the temperature falls fast and you would freeze to death just a few kilometres up.

OLD TIMER

Planet Earth is roughly a third of the age of the Universe (making Earth about 4·5 billion years old).

The Earth is carrying you with it round the Sun at 107,000 km/h.

251 million years ago, most species (kinds) of living thing died out, including 96% of all water species and 70% of land species. No one is sure why this happened.

If you travelled back to a time before life existed on Earth, you would be killed by the deadly atmosphere. Without plants, the air would still be unbreathable today.

Ripley's Believe It or Not!®

No one knows exactly how many individual living things there are on Earth, but it is at least 5 million trillion trillion – almost all of which are too small to see without a microscope.

5 MILLION TRILLION TRILLION IS WRITTEN LIKE THIS 5,000,000,000,000,000,000,000,000,000,000 **THAT'S A WHOLE LOT OF ZEROS!**

...THE EARTH

* Diameter: 12,742 km (on average)
* Mass: 6 trillion trillion kg
* Goes around the Sun in: one year (365.24 days)
* Spins on its axis in: 24 hours
* Made mostly of: iron
* Atmosphere made mostly of: nitrogen

>>all around the world>>

40-year-old Jason Lewis from Britain was the first man to travel around the world using only muscle power. It took him 13 years to complete the journey on roller blades, bicycle and a pedal-powered boat on his 'Expedition 360'.

Photographs taken by satellites and from the International Space Station (ISS) show huge differences in the landscapes around our planet.

If all the ice on the Earth melted, the sea would rise by 100 m.

The Earth's Poles are about 21 km closer to the centre of the Earth than the Equator.

If you stood on the Earth's Equator, you would be spinning around with the Earth at 1670 km/h.

SAY WHAT?

POLES
The 'ends' of a planet, around which it spins.

Our sensational Star

THE SUN

The Earth seems like a pretty gigantic place, but compared to the Sun it's nothing to brag about. The Sun is literally massive – 333,000 times the Earth's mass. This bulk is what makes the Sun shine – deep inside, the pressure is so enormous that nuclear reactions take place, like billions of nuclear weapons going off every second.

Even though the surface of the Sun is much cooler than the core, it's still 6,050°C: so hot that any metal on Earth would melt there. Yet, despite all that, the Sun is a very dull and ordinary star, like many of those in the sky. It is only the fact that it is 250,000 times closer to Earth than the next nearest star that makes it seem so bright.

The Sun is about one-third as old as the Universe, and about halfway through its life.

The Sun sometimes ejects (throws out) plasma. This is called a coronal mass ejection (CME).

If it were not for the Sun, Earth's surface temperature would be about −270°C.

The Earth could fit inside the Sun 1.3 million times!

Shown here is the approximate size of Earth in comparison with the Sun.

THE SUN

If the Sun suddenly vanished, we would see it in the sky for another eight minutes. This is the time it takes for sunlight to reach the Earth.

When the Sun begins to run out of fuel, it will grow so large and hot that it will melt the surface of the Earth.

The element helium was discovered on the Sun before it was found on Earth.

In 840, Emperor Louis of Bavaria died of fright caused by experiencing an eclipse of the Sun.

The Sun gives out enough energy in one second to supply the USA with energy for 50 million years! To produce this, it burns up an incredible 4 million tonnes of its mass. However, it will take about 5 billion years to burn it all up, so we needn't worry about it running out.

The Sun is 400 times bigger than our Moon but also 400 times farther away from the Earth.

The Sun outweighs the Earth by the same amount as 175 Boeing 747 planes to one person.

twist it!

Ripley's Believe It or Not!®

A pinhead-sized speck of the burning gases from our Sun could kill a man from 160 km away.

SAY WHAT?

ELEMENT

One of about 100 basic substances from which everything is made.

>>solar power>>

By harnessing the power of the Sun, a family in Montana, USA, spends only $20 a month on their fuel bills. Their aim was to build an environmentally friendly house without spending a fortune; 250 old tyres and 13,000 empty drinks cans were used in the building!

Blackout

If the Moon moves between the Earth and the Sun, a solar eclipse occurs. Total eclipses are rare, and don't last long – usually less than seven minutes. In 1973 passengers on Concorde flew along with the Moon's moving umbra (shadow) and watched the eclipse for 74 minutes!

Lunar Tunes

IN THE KNOW...

...OUR MOON

* Average distance from Earth: 384,000 km
* Average diameter: 27% Earth
* Mass: 1.2% of Earth
* Length of day: 27 Earth days

It's around 384,000 km away in space, but the Moon is the Earth's nearest neighbour – though it's as far away from home as humans have managed to get. It is an airless, lifeless ball of rocky mountains and plains of old lava but its effect on the Earth is massive – literally. Together with the Sun, it moves billions of tonnes of water each day, making the tides that wash every shore.

There are dozens of seas on the Moon, but no liquid water. The seas are areas of solidified lava (melted rock).

The beginning of the Moon was almost the end of the Earth: about 4.5 billion years ago, a planet-sized object smashed into our newly born world, and fragments from both planets made the Moon. If the object had been a little bigger, you wouldn't be here to read about it.

The Moon is getting farther away from you all the time; each full moon is about 2 mm further away than the last one.

Ripley's Believe It or Not!®

Because there is no weather on the Moon, astronauts' footprints will survive for decades.

twist it!

FULL OF MOONS

The far side of the Moon was not seen until 1959, when a spacecraft sent a photo of it back to Earth. The Moon turns as it circles the Earth, always keeping the same face toward us.

In 1968, Russian tortoises flew around the Moon before returning safely to Earth in the Zond 5 spaceship.

The Moon contains mysterious areas called 'mascons', which generate gravity strong enough to pull satellites off course.

If something happens 'once in a blue moon', it could be more often than you think: a blue moon is the second of two full moons in one month, and occurs about once every 2¾ years. Don't get too excited – the Moon doesn't actually change colour!

Wish you were here!

The US has successfully put people on the Moon six times. The first was in 1969 and the last was in 1972. Twelve astronauts have walked on the surface. Neil Armstrong was the first person to set foot on the Moon.

The massive costs involved in putting people on the Moon have prevented further government-funded missions. However, the Google Lunar X Prize offers $20 million to the first privately funded team to land a robotic probe on the Moon.

GLITTER BALL

In 1992 the *Galileo* spacecraft, on its way to Jupiter, took pictures of the Moon using special colour filters to record different substances making up the surface. When all the images are put together they give quite a different view – something more like a festive decoration than the Moon we see at night!

GETTING AWAY FROM IT ALL

Dutch architect Hans-Jurgen Rombaut has designed the first hotel intended for the Moon. It is supposed to be finished by 2050 and will have two tall, thin towers, extra-thick walls, and an insulating layer of water to keep out dangerous cosmic rays and regulate the temperature indoors.

HellPlanets

MERCURY AND VENUS

Imagine a world where the Sun is six times brighter than usual, the sky is black, and the weather is hot enough to melt lead during the day and colder than a freezer at night. There is almost no air at all... This is what it is like on Mercury, the closest planet to our Sun.

MERCURY

The largest crater in the Solar System is on Mercury. It is 643 km across and called Beethoven.

On Mercury, a day lasts longer than a year.

Ripley's Believe It or Not!®

Seen from some parts of Mercury, the Sun rises twice a day at some times of the year. If you lived there, you would see the Sun rise about halfway up the sky, then reverse direction and set, before rising again and passing across the sky as usual.

IN THE KNOW...

...MERCURY

* Average distance from Sun: 58 million km
* Diameter: 38% of Earth
* Mass: 5% of Earth
* Length of year: 88 Earth days
* Length of day: 176 Earth days

The first space probe to visit two planets, *Mariner 10* zoomed past Venus in 1974. It used the gravitational pull of Venus to change its orbit and head off to Mercury. Over 30 years later, *Messenger* has become only the second spacecraft to send back data about Mercury.

...VENUS

Average distance from Sun: 108 million km

Diameter: 95% of Earth

Mass: 82% of Earth

Length of year: 225 Earth days

Length of day: 117 Earth days

The highest volcano on Venus is called Maat Mons, and it rises 8 km above the planet's surface. It is named after the Egyptian goddess of justice and truth. Every surface feature on Venus is named after a female, with just three exceptions.

>> *Messenger* was launched on the night of 3 August 2004. >>

Though farther from the Sun than Mercury, **Venus is even hotter (about 460°C), because it is blanketed by a thick atmosphere. Without protection, you would die quickly, and not just from the heat: on Venus the air is deadly. Conditions on Venus are so extreme that no space probe that has managed to land there has survived for more than a few hours.**

VENUS

twist it!

The rain on Venus is made of sulphuric acid — but it boils away before it reaches the ground.

Venus has more dry land than anywhere else in the Solar System.

Venus spins backwards, so the Sun rises in the West there — or it would if it were not too cloudy to see it.

On Venus, the sky is orange. On Mercury, it is black.

TOTALLY OUT THERE

SAY WHAT?

SULPHURIC ACID *Dangerous liquid which 'eats away' many materials.*

Red Planet

🜨 MARS

Mars is a harsh world of deserts and dust, red with rusted iron, but it would still win a 'most similar planet to Earth' competition, with its icy poles, seasons and 24.6-hour day. It used to be even more like home, with a thick atmosphere. Rivers once ran across the surface – and maybe living creatures did, too.

Since *Mariner 4* flew past in 1965, over 40 probes have been sent to explore Mars (more than to any other planet), and it is the next destination for human explorers. Despite the thin air on Mars, it does have weather – clouds, frost and dust-storms – but the last rainy day there was more than a million years ago.

Scientists use 3-D pictures like this one of the North Pole of Mars to work out the amount of water or ice there, and to study the surface and clouds.

MARS

In the 19th century, creatures from Mars were usually called Martians.

Dust storms on Mars sometimes cover the whole planet.

On Mars, the sky is pink.

Viking 1 landed here in 1976 and took photos of the surface of Mars.

Planet GIANTS

JUPITER AND SATURN

Jupiter and Saturn are the overweight giants of the Solar System – Jupiter is heavier than all the other planets put together. It has an enormously deep atmosphere full of multicoloured storm clouds. It has 63 moons and is surrounded by a system of rings made of millions of pieces of rock.

Jupiter gives out more heat than it gets from the Sun.

In 1609, Italian scientist and astronomer Galileo Galilei used his new telescope to discover the four largest of Jupiter's moons.

Many of Jupiter's moons orbit in the opposite direction to the planet's spin.

Europa, a moon of Jupiter, is the smoothest world we know, with no hills or valleys.

Jupiter's Red Spot is a hurricane that has lasted for centuries. It is the biggest storm in the Solar System.

The Red Spot is 24,800 km across – almost twice as wide as Earth. Wind speeds inside the storm reach 435 km/h.

Ripley's Believe It or Not!®

Volcanoes on Jupiter's moon Io can spew out hot material at speeds of 1 km/second. That's 20 times faster than the average volcano on Earth.

Io is the most volcanic place in the Solar System.

IN THE KNOW...
...JUPITER

* Average distance from Sun: 778 million km
* Average diameter: 10.9 times Earth
* Mass: 318 times Earth
* Length of year: 12 Earth years
* Length of day: 9.9 hours

The Earth could fit inside Saturn 1,321 times over. Like Jupiter, Saturn is shrouded by clouds, and no one knows exactly what lies beneath. It has many moons (about 61) including a weird cloudy moon called Titan, with air like car exhausts and, at least in places, a soft surface with a crispy coating. Saturn is famous for the rocky rings that surround it.

SATURN

...IN THE KNOW...

...SATURN

* Average distance from Sun: 1,427 million km
* Average diameter: 9 times Earth
* Mass: 95 times Earth
* Length of year: 29.5 Earth years
* Length of day: 10.7 hours

Saturn is so light it would float in your bath (if you had a bath bigger than a planet, that is).

Some of Saturn's rings are kept in place by objects like small moons, called shepherds.

In 1610, Galileo discovered Saturn. His telescope wasn't good enough to see the rings properly and he thought they were moons. The next time he looked, they had disappeared! At a certain angle, the rings are 'edge on' and so are hardly visible.

Saturn is about twice as far from the Sun as Jupiter is.

>> double shift >>

In 2008, the Cassini spacecraft completed its four-year mission to explore the Saturn system. It was still in good working order, so it was given a new 'Equinox' mission, which will give scientists two more years to make more in-depth studies of Saturn and its rings.

IceWorlds

🌀 URANUS, NEPTUNE AND PLUTO

Uranus is an ice giant. It is so far from the Sun that it is always colder there than the coldest Earth winter: about –200°C. A greeny blue planet, it spins on its side following a collision (crash) with an unknown object billions of years ago.

Neptune is also huge and cold, about –210°C, and the fastest winds in the Solar System (over 2,000 km/h). It is blue, with white clouds and the

NEPTUNE

"From Neptune, the Sun looks 1,960 times dimmer than it does from Earth."

IN THE KNOW...

...NEPTUNE

✳ Average distance from Sun: 4,497 million km
✳ Average diameter: 3.9 times Earth
✳ Mass: 17 times Earth
✳ Length of year: 165 Earth years
✳ Length of day: 16.1 hours

Triton is Neptune's largest moon. It has active volcanoes, though it is the coldest world we know. The volcanoes are made of nitrogen.

There are places on Uranus where night lasts more than 40 Earth years.

URANUS

"When William Herschel first discovered Uranus, he thought it was a comet."

IN THE KNOW...

...URANUS

✳ Average distance from Sun: 2,871 million km
✳ Average diameter: 4 times Earth
✳ Mass: 15 times Earth
✳ Length of year: 84 Earth years
✳ Length of day: 17.2 hours

FAR OUT

The ice giants are so dim that Uranus was only discovered by accident in 1781.

Neptune, the outermost planet in the Solar System, was tracked down through the effect of its gravity on the way Uranus moved, and not found until 1846.

If you visited either of these planets and looked back towards the Sun, it would simply look like a bright star.

William Herschel wanted to call Uranus 'George's Star', in honour of the king, George III.

Neptune is so far from the Sun that it takes 165 Earth years to make one orbit, so if you were born there, you would not live long enough to celebrate your first birthday.

Neptune has still not been around the Sun once since it was discovered in 1846. It will finally complete its first orbit on 8 June 2011.

twist it!

If you can't imagine Uranus spinning on its side (rather than like a spinning top, like the other planets) then try to imagine it like a ball rolling along.

PLUTO

Pluto used to be called a planet, but is now officially a humble dwarf planet, one of three discovered so far. It usually orbits the Sun outside Neptune and is even colder, and mostly covered with frozen nitrogen gas.

- Pluto spins on its side, in a similar way to Uranus.

- Pluto was the ninth planet of our Solar System until the 2006 discovery of Eris, which forced astronomers to create a new definition of a true planet. The three dwarf planets are Pluto, Eris and Ceres.

- Pluto's orbit isn't as circular as Neptune's, so although it is usually farther from the Sun, sometimes it changes position! Its orbit crosses inside that of Neptune for about 20 years in every 248.

- The coldest place on Earth (in Antarctica) has an average temperature about four times higher than Pluto's daytime temperature. Brrr!

>>new horizons>>

A spacecraft called New Horizons is on its way to Pluto. It was the fastest spacecraft ever launched, travelling at about 16 km/second soon after it blasted off in 2006. It passed Jupiter in 2007 and is due to reach Pluto in 2015. It will be the first ever spacecraft to study Pluto.

Danger Zone

Comets are like giant dirty snowballs. Usually comets are pretty happy orbiting far out at the edge of the Solar System, about seven trillion kilometres from Earth, but sometimes they swoop in towards the Sun, growing tails of gas and dust as they warm up.

If you've ever seen a comet, you probably weren't afraid – after all, it was just a whitish streak in the sky. Don't be fooled, though: comets can kill. In fact, it was probably a comet (or perhaps an asteroid) that wiped out the mighty dinosaurs 65 million years ago. It crashed into the Earth and the dust it threw up froze the planet, which killed the dinosaurs. And it could happen again – to us.

SAY WHAT?

ASTEROID
A small rocky body in orbit around the Sun. Many asteroids are located between the orbits of Mars and Jupiter. These are the building blocks of a planet that failed to form there.

In 2000, Comet Hyakutake had a tail 550 million km long – nearly four times longer than the distance from the Earth to the Sun!

Whooosh...

The centre of a comet is called its nucleus.

amazing!!

This colossal crater, seen here from space, in Australia's Northern Territory is called Gosses Bluff and is about 4.5 km wide. It was made by an asteroid or comet about 1 km across that crashed into Earth around 142 million years ago.

Comets are made of ice, dust and rocky material that came from the Solar System when it was first created about 4.5 billion years ago.

Ripley's Believe It or Not!®

Most comets have two streaming tails – a blue one made of gas and a white one made of dust.

twist it!

A comet or asteroid the size of a city crashed into Mexico's Yucatan Peninsula 65 million years ago.

A comet called Shoemaker-Levy 9 crashed into Jupiter in 1994. It hit the planet on the side that was facing away from Earth, so the impact itself wasn't seen, but huge marks could be seen in Jupiter's atmosphere for several months afterwards.

Halley is a comet that reappears every 75.3 years. There are records of its visits that go back to 25 May, 240BC.

If you had been around in 1910, when the Earth passed through the tail of a comet, you could have tried some of the anti-comet pills that were on sale. But they wouldn't have done you any good!

In 1908, a strange explosion flattened 2,150 sq km of forest in Siberia. It was probably caused by a comet exploding in the air.

WATCH IT!

Rubbish!

SPACE RUBBLE AND JUNK

Building a solar system isn't a tidy job: after gravity pulled together our Sun and the planets, trillions of grains of dust and lumps of rock were left hanging about in space. There is a ring of scattered rubble between Mars and Jupiter called the asteroid belt, and even more rubble beyond Neptune.

Most of this rubble keeps itself to itself, but some of it falls through our atmosphere. If it is small enough, it drifts down to Earth and just makes everything a bit dustier. Bigger chunks burn up as meteors (shooting stars), and a few reach the ground as meteorites.

There are thousands of pieces of space junk in orbit around Earth. Space junk includes items such as broken satellites, parts of rockets, and even rubbish thrown from space staions. There are also around 6,000 artificial satellites.

The first TV satellite was launched in 1964 to allow the Tokyo Olympics to be transmitted around the world.

This artist's impression shows all the satellites (drawn larger than actual size) orbiting Earth.

Ripley's Believe It or Not!®

Think you've seen a flying saucer? It could just be the reflection of the Sun off a satellite!

METEORIC!

The *Skylab* space station created a spectacular meteor shower over Australia when it crashed to Earth in 1979.

The oldest man-made debris hurtling around our planet is the US satellite *Vanguard*. It was launched in 1958 and is still up there today.

For centuries, people living in Greenland made their tools out of three large meteorites, which were almost pure iron.

Asteroids were once thought to be fragments of an exploded planet.

About 500 meteorites crash to Earth each year, but only about five of these are found and reported to scientists. So you'll be fairly famous if you find one and hand it in.

Some meteorites began life on the Moon or Mars and were thrown into space by volcanoes before drifting through space to land on Earth.

twist it!

ACTUAL SIZE!

Scientists have only three rock samples from other objects in our Solar System – they are from the Moon, Mars and this piece of the asteroid Vesta, which fell to Earth as a meteorite.

Mrs Hewlett Hodges from Alabama, USA, has actually been hit by a meteorite! It crashed through her roof, bounced off a radio and hit her on the hip. Ouch!

>>shooting from the hip>>

TRASH CRASH

The first major collision between two satellites happened in February 2009, when an old Russian satellite crashed into a working US satellite and created at least 600 more pieces of space junk.

LETHAL CLOTHING

In 1965 the US astronaut Edward White lost a glove while on a space walk from Gemini 4. It remained in orbit for a month, reaching speeds of 28,000 km/h, and posed a lethal danger to spacecraft.

PUTTING OUT THE TRASH

The Mir space station threw more than 200 rubbish bags into space over ten years. They are all still in orbit.

POW!

Space junk travels extremely fast, which makes it highly dangerous. At a speed of 27,400 km/h a tiny speck hitting an astronaut on a space walk would have the same impact as a bullet.

Looking Up

How many stars do you think you can see in the night sky? A million? A billion? Actually, even on the darkest, clearest night, fewer than 3,000 are visible. This is only a tiny fraction of the mind-numbing total number, which is at least 70 billion trillion – said to be more than all the grains of sand on all the beaches in the world.

Some stars you can see are as big and bright as our Sun – and some are much bigger. Many stars are double, each spinning around the other. Many stars have planets, too. Stars usually last for billions of years – but the more massive they are, the brighter they burn and the shorter they live.

These stars make up one of the most massive star clusters in the Milky Way galaxy.

THIS STAR CLUSTER IS HIDDEN FROM SIGHT BY INTERSTELLAR DUST, BUT CAN BE SEEN WITH INFRARED TELESCOPES.

This is the remains of a supernova explosion (see page 30).

Ripley's Believe It or Not!®

Seeing double

About half of the stars in the Universe exist in pairs. They are called binary stars, and both orbit around the same point.

The red stars are supergiants, and the blue ones are young or newly formed stars.

ORION

CANIS MAJOR

GEMINI

TAURUS

Constellations are groups of stars that, from the Earth, look close to each other. They may really be huge distances apart in space, but they line up to form patterns that have been given names through history.

Orion, or The Hunter, is instantly recognisable by the three central stars making his 'belt'.

Canis Major, one of Orion's 'hunting dogs', contains Sirius, the brightest star in our sky. It is about 25 times brighter than the Sun.

The constellation of **Gemini** is one of the signs of the zodiac. It looks like a pair of twins and can be seen around the world between December and March.

Taurus is also known as The Bull. It contains the Pleiades (say 'ply-uh-dees') star cluster and is visible between November and February.

>> star light, star bright >>

Scientists think that new stars are formed inside nebulae (the plural of a nebula) such as this one. A nebula is a cloud full of dust and gas; when it gets squashed, parts of it get so hot that they become newborn stars.

twist it

The light from most stars you can see takes decades to get to the Earth – which means you are seeing them as they were before you were born.

Some brown dwarf stars are cooler than burning houses.

The star with the longest name is Shurnarkabtishashutu, which is Arabic for 'under the southern horn of the bull'.

If the Earth were the size of a marble, the nearest star would be 30,000 km away.

The largest known star, VV Canis Majoris, is large enough to contain about 100 billion objects the size of the Sun.

STAR TURNS

Celebrities as diverse as Britney Spears, Harrison Ford, Bruce Lee and even the whole of Arsenal FC have had stars named for them! Scientists give stars a name made up of letters and numbers (such as HD172167) but fans and celebrities themselves can pay to have their name given to a specific star.

Star Death

When the Sun runs out of fuel, it will swell up and melt the Earth's surface – but there's no rush to leave home; it won't happen until about the year 5,000,000,000. Stars more than five times as massive as the Sun explode as supernovas, shining more brightly than a whole galaxy of stars.

Supernovas leave behind shrunken remains, and sometimes those remains are black holes. Why are they black even suck in light – nothing in the Universe can escape them. Not that you would need to worry about escaping – you'd be torn apart by the strong gravity well before you reached the hole itself.

This jet is lots of high-energy particles being blasted away by the black hole.

✳ The black hole at the centre of this galaxy (called Centaurus A) has a mass one billion times more than our Sun.

✳ Centaurus A is really two galaxies in collision – and it is full of new stars that are forming as a result. Trillions of tonnes of material from both galaxies is gradually being sucked into the black hole.

✳ Scientists can study this black hole and galaxy more easily than many others as it is relatively close to the Earth. It is about 14 million light-years from us, which means that the light from Centaurus A takes about 14 million years to reach us. One light year is about 10 trillion km.

>>10 billion+ years in the life of our Sun! >>

5 BILLION YEARS AGO
Nebula shrinks under its own gravity and stars begin to form

PROTOSTAR: temperature rises, nuclear reactions start inside to stabilize star

TODAY
Our Sun provides heat and light to the Earth

GETTING HOTTER
Sun gets brighter and hotter (10% hotter every billion years)

Some of your body was formed in a supernova: to be precise, all the atoms of carbon and oxygen inside you.

A supernova was seen by Chinese astronomers in AD1054. Actually, it exploded in about 4000BC, but the light took 5,000 years to get here.

It is just possible that spinning black holes might allow astronauts in the far future to travel back in time.

A supernova releases more energy over a few months than the Sun will over its entire lifetime.

Supernovas can cause the birth of new stars and planets when their explosions disturb nearby dust clouds.

Supernovas can also be caused by one star dumping material onto a companion star.

twist it!

Ripley's Believe It or Not!®

YOU DO THE MATH!

After some stars run out of fuel and collapse, what is left of them is a shrunken massive object called a neutron star, where the gravity is so strong that you would weigh over 100,000 million kg there.

A single spoonful of material from a neutron star would weigh a billion tonnes on Earth!

Neutron stars are so compressed that they squeeze a tenth of the matter that made up the original giant star (before it imploded) into a ball that is 1.5 billion times smaller.

Some neutron stars send beams of radio waves sweeping through space. If they sweep across the Earth, the radio waves can be detected as short pulses. Neutron stars like this are called pulsars.

STARTING SOMETHING

This picture of a supernova remnant was taken by the Hubble Space Telescope (see page 35). It is made up of gas and dust. In a few million years, it could form new planets around a sun-like star, like the beginnings of our Solar System.

SAY WHAT?

ATOMS
Tiny objects, much too small to see. All solids, liquids and gases are made of them.

5 BILLION YEARS FROM NOW	RED GIANT:	PLANETARY NEBULA:	WHITE DWARF:	BLACK DWARF:
Sun's core collapses and outer layers spread out	Sun swallows up Mercury, Venus and maybe Earth	Sun throws off a cloud of gas	nebula cools and fades	Sun is no longer visible

Getting Together

Stars are gathered together throughout the Universe in groups called galaxies. Our own one is the Milky Way and it is made of about 300 billion stars (give or take a hundred billion) – so all the stars you can see on the darkest night add up to less than 0.000001% (or one-ten-millionth) of the whole thing.

Last century, astronomers noticed something very odd – most other galaxies are hurtling away from ours, and from each other too. They realised that the whole Universe is getting bigger every second, and that everything in the Universe must have been crunched up together long ago. Very, very long ago (13.7 billion years to be precise), when it all began as a sudden expansion – the Big Bang.

- Our Solar System is perched between two arms of the Milky Way.

- If you counted one star a second and never slept, it would still take you about 3,000 years to count the stars in our galaxy.

- Long ago, most galaxies were blue, because of all the young stars being born in them.

- There are different types of galaxy, named according to their shape. The Milky Way is a spiral galaxy – it's not hard to see why.

NO PLACE LIKE HOME

twist it!

Our Solar System is here.

INTO GALACTIC

The nearest large galaxy to the Milky Way is the Andromeda galaxy: it is so far away that its light takes 2.5 million years to reach us, and it is the furthest thing you can see with your naked eye.

Our galaxy is on a collision course with the Andromeda galaxy, but the galaxies won't meet until after our Sun has died.

You, along with the rest of our galaxy, are being dragged through space at about 2 million km an hour by a mysterious unknown object called the Great Attractor. It's hidden from us by dust clouds.

It takes about 225 million years for our Sun to revolve (move in a circle) once around the centre of the galaxy.

the Milky Way

The Milky Way looks brighter from the Southern Hemisphere, because the southern part of our planet points roughly towards the star-packed centre of our Galaxy. We live out in the suburbs, near the galactic edge, and can look out on the stars around us. If we lived near the centre, the sky would be packed with stars, and the starlight would be brighter than the light of the full Moon. But, as there is a massive black hole in those parts, you might not have long to enjoy the view.

>>what happens next?>>

Most scientists think the expansion will go on for ever, even after the stars have all died and the Universe is cold. They call this the Big Chill. But some scientists think that, in about the year 50,000,000,000, everything will fall apart. First galaxies will be torn apart, then stars, then planets, then you (if you're still around, which is a bit unlikely) and finally atoms — the Big Rip.

BIG BANG FACTS

Astronomers see back to almost the beginning of time when they look at quasars. Quasars are very bright objects (caused by various things falling into supermassive black holes) that can be seen across vast distances. To cross those distances, their light takes nearly as long as the age of the Universe.

For hundreds of thousands of years after it formed, the Universe was dark.

The Big Bang wasn't an explosion — space was only created when it happened, so there was nowhere for it to explode into!

The Universe is more than a hundred million times older than the oldest person.

The most distant objects in the Universe are moving away from us at over 280,000 km/second.

Most of the atoms in your body are hydrogen, which formed very soon after the Big Bang — so most of you is almost as old as the Universe.

Star Gazing

TELESCOPES

Telescopes allow astronomers to see objects so far away that their light takes billions of years to reach us. Many telescopes gather light using huge mirrors, which is then focused by a lens. Some of these mirrors are ten million times the size of your pupils, which are what you use to gather light. They can collect light for hours on end (which your eyes can't).

There are also telescopes that detect 'light' that we can't see at all – like radio waves, infra-red, ultraviolet, X-rays and gamma rays. So, if you want to have a good look round outer space, take some advice – use a telescope.

These are the 'Pillars of Creation' – huge pillars of space dust lit by new stars.

This orange disc is the dying remains of a huge star, which exploded thousands of years ago.

The 'Trifid Nebula' is a giant cloud of gas and dust where stars form.

These images were all obtained by the Spitzer Space Telescope.

The top of Mauna Kea (a volcano in Hawaii) is home to 13 telescopes owned and run by astronomers from 11 countries (including Japan, Canada, France, the UK and the USA). The site has more cloud-free nights than most other suitable places around the world.

This is Mauna Loa, the world's largest volcano.

The most powerful telescopes can see so far away, the light started travelling billions of years ago. They show us galaxies as they looked less than one billion years after the beginning of the Universe.

The largest radio telescope dish in the world is at Arecibo, Puerto Rico. It is 305 m across.

Italian scientist Galileo Galilei built one of the first telescopes in 1609. Within a few nights he had discovered mountains on the Moon, four moons of Jupiter and hundreds of unknown stars.

The nearest star is about one million times further from Earth than the nearest planet.

The highest speed in the Universe is the speed of light, which is 299,792 km/second. It would take over four years to reach the nearest star even at this speed. But don't bother trying to go that fast – the faster you go, the more massive you get, and you would weigh more than the Universe by the time you got close to light speed.

twist it!

Ripley's Believe It or Not!®

The Hubble Space Telescope (HST) orbits the Earth so that its view of the Universe is not interrupted by the atmosphere (like ground-based telescopes). It can see a coin 700 km away!

SAY WHAT?

PUPIL
The dark hole in the middle of each eye, through which light enters.

STARING INTO SPACE

The Spitzer Space Telescope was launched in 2003 and orbits the Earth, taking infrared pictures to help scientists study how galaxies are formed and develop. Infrared is heat radiation, so the telescope has to be kept cool so that its own heat doesn't interfere with the signals it receives from space.

The **Very Large Array (VLA)** is an arrangement of 27 large radio telescopes in New Mexico, USA. Each one measures 25 m across (about the size of a house). They are all mounted on tracks so they can be moved into different positions, but work together to act like one large radio telescope.

VERY LARGE INDEED

Observatories with telescopes inside.

Saturn V Rocket

Saturn V Rocket

As tall as St Paul's Cathedral in London; higher than the Statue of Liberty!

111 m tall (including Apollo spacecraft).

Into the Unknown

THE 'SPACE RACE'

Looking at the stars, it's hard to imagine what it's like in space. Telescopes allow us to see what's up there in much more detail. But there's nothing like getting up close and personal, and that's what the invention of spaceships has done for humans – and for the various animals that have been blasted into space for research purposes.

The first space orbit was by the Russian artificial satellite, Sputnik, in 1957. The first human in space was also Russian, Yuri Gagarin, who orbited the Earth in 1961. The rivalry between the USA and Russia (then called the Soviet Union) drove both countries on in the 'Space Race' to achieve milestones in all areas of space exploration. Many people think that putting man on the Moon, in 1969, made the US the ultimate winners. Nowadays, international cooperation allows us to find out more about our Universe than ever before.

...SATURN V

...IN THE KNOW...

First manned flight: December, 1968

Last flight: December, 1972

Total launches: 13

Total made: 15 (2 were unused)

The Saturn V rockets used to launch the Apollo craft on their Moon missions were the biggest and most powerful launch vehicles ever used.

- Each Saturn V rocket carried enough fuel to fill an Olympic swimming pool, and used it up in 2.5 minutes.

- There were three stages in a Saturn V rocket. Each stage separated and fell away after use. The third stage fired twice: to enter orbit and to change its path to head toward the Moon.

10 m across.

The 2008 movie Space Chimps was based on a true story! Well, kind of – the main character, Ham III, is the supposed grandson of a real chimp called Ham, who was launched into space in 1961. Ham was sent up in a *Project Mercury* capsule as part of the research needed for human space travel. He landed successfully in the ocean after the flight, and lived until 1983 at North Carolina Zoo.

Ripley's Believe It or Not!®

>> FIRSTS >>

In 1961, Yuri Gagarin (USSR) became the first human being ever in space, and the first to orbit the Earth. The first people to see him upon his return were two Russian farm workers, Anna and Rita Takhtarov, who must have been quite surprised to see him emerge into a field from his landing craft.

The Russian *Soyuz* series of spacecraft first flew in 1966 and is still operating today, carrying astronauts to the International Space Station. *Soyuz* rockets have launched more human spaceflight missions than any other space program.

To Boldly Go

EXPLORATION

All modern spaceships are launched from Earth using liquid-fuelled rockets. The first of these took off in 1926 and reached a height of 12 m. Impressive? No, but 43 years later, a liquid fuel rocket carried three men 30,000 times further – to the Moon. The 1960s and 1970s was an era of giant rockets, with giant pricetags, and they could be used only once. From the 1980s a cheaper vehicle has been used and re-used: the space shuttle.

A space shuttle does exactly what it says – shuttles satellites to space and people to the International Space Station (ISS). Russian Soyuz spacecraft go there, too, and one Soyuz craft is always docked at the ISS just in case an emergency getaway is needed.

The spent fuel tank falls away.

The shuttle lands back on Earth.

The space shuttle blasts off.

KEY FACTS

- After launch, the shuttle starts to twist into an arc ready to enter orbit.
- 126 seconds after launch, the thin white rocket boosters are pushed away from the shuttle.
- Next, the brown fuel tank falls away and burns up as it re-enters the Earth's atmosphere.
- When the mission ends, the shuttle orbiter glides back to Earth and lands like an aeroplane.

External fuel tank

Solid Rocket Booster (SRB)

Cockpit

Orbiter

United States

Atlantis

<< **BLAST OFF!** >>

The first rocket flight in 1926 was of a liquid-fuelled rocket invented by Robert Goddard of Massachusetts, USA. He launched it on his Aunt Effie's farm and after reaching 12 m, it landed in a cabbage field.

HITCHING A RIDE

Ripley's Believe It or Not!®

After landing, the space shuttle orbiter is fastened onto the back of a Boeing 747 plane to be flown back to the launch site, ready for its next mission.

Elevons for control

Engine nozzle

Rudder

In 2009, a bat blasted off on the side of space shuttle *Discovery*'s external tank. No one knows how long it managed to hold on for.

A 1995 space-shuttle launch was delayed by woodpeckers, who pecked holes in its fuel tank.

twist it!

The humble flea can accelerate about 50 times faster.

The engine that powers a space shuttle is as powerful as 39 train engines, yet is only one-seventh of the weight. In 25 seconds it can pump enough fuel to fill a swimming pool, and the overall power of a space shuttle at takeoff is equivalent to 16 million horsepower. Despite this,

The fastest humans were the astronauts on the *Apollo 10* mission, who reached 39,897 km/h on their way back to Earth in 1969.

Once they're well away from Earth and other large objects, spaceships can keep moving without using any fuel at all.

The first space traveller was a dog called Laika, who was sent into space in 1957.

England's 'Astronomer Royal' said in 1956 that 'Space travel is utter bilge'. The first satellite was launched the following year. How embarrassing!

5-4-3-2-1

Sky Workers

'Backpack' contains breathable oxygen.

Each mission has its own insignia (logo) on a badge.

Jet pack allows astronaut to fly back to International Space Station (ISS) in an emergency.

Inner suit (like underwear) is temperature controlled.

SUITS YOU!

Legs and arms have special suit joints to allow more movement.

Boots have metal rings at the top to alter their size for different astronauts.

Space is a dangerous place: there's no air there, and it's full of deadly radiation. In the sunlight, it's hotter than an oven; in the shadows it's colder than a freezer. An unprotected person would be dead in seconds.

So, to venture into space, people have to be sealed into spacesuits, and the suits have to be warmed, cooled, pressurised and supplied with fresh air. It's no wonder that a spacesuit takes over six hours to put on, and costs well over a million dollars.

➤ Living in weightless conditions for weeks and months takes its toll on the human body. Astronauts have to exercise every day to keep their muscles strong.

➤ It can be tricky using a toolbox in space – your screwdriver floats away! To help with ordinary maintenance, astronauts use velcro belts to keep their tools on hand, and hook their feet under straps or bars to stop themselves from drifting around.

➤ Astronauts only wear special spacesuits for take off and landing, or when they leave the ISS. The rest of the time, they wear normal clothes like shorts and T-shirts.

Astronauts wear this orange suit for launch and landing. It's called an LES: Launch and Entry Suit.

Space Diary

Get up at 6am GMT. We're allowed 90 minutes' 'post-sleep' to wash, dress, eat breakfast, maybe exercise, and be ready to start work.

DPC (daily planning conference) with ground control centre for 15 mins, to confirm the day's actions. My job today is unpacking supplies brought by the shuttle. I think tomorrow will be science experiments, and at the weekend I get time to myself. Will hook up with my family on a video link (until the signal dies!). Most mornings I manage to use the treadmill or the exercise bike, too.

Lunch break is an hour, and the crew all eat together. Warm up my food and take the chance to take photos out of the Service Module windows. Earth looks amazing from up here!

More ground support links in the afternoon to check that all is going to plan. Have to do our chores even up in space! We have a new toilet system for one of the guys to activate, and I need to finish that unpacking. Everything has its proper place!

Finish work at 6pm and unwind over dinner with the others. Time to catch up on some reading, emails or just gazing at the views. We have movies for the weekends, and tuck ourselves into bed about 9.30 (although sometimes we stay up later!).

It isn't easy using the toilet in space! The waste gets sucked away and put in bags for disposal. On spacewalks, astronauts wear adult nappies as they can be outside the ISS for hours.

When it's bedtime, astronauts climb into sleeping bags, which are fixed to the wall, and hook their arms into restraints to stop them from floating around in their sleep.

Astronauts often wash with a damp cloth to reduce the amount of water used on the ISS.

Food is often warmed in a microwave and eaten from a special tray that stops everything from floating away.

twist it!

Half of all space-travellers get space-sick.

Astronauts grow 5 cm when they are in space, because their backbones are no longer squashed by the Earth's gravity.

The longest spacewalk was in 1992 and took 8 hours and 29 minutes. It was made by shuttle astronauts who were dealing with a faulty satellite.

In 2001, orbiting astronauts took delivery of a pizza! It wasn't delivered by a person on a moped though...

Astronauts can't shed tears in space, so it's an ideal place to peel onions!

If you were an astronaut in orbit, you would see the Sun rise and set 15 times a day, because of your speedy motion around the Earth.

There is no up (and no down) in space.

SPACED OUT

Ripley's Believe It or Not!®

During a spacewalk to retrieve two broken satellites, American astronaut Dale Gardner had his photo taken offering to sell them to anyone interested! The picture was taken by his fellow astronaut Joseph Allen, who can be seen in the reflection on Gardner's visor.

FOR SALE

SPACE AGE

John Glenn was the first American to orbit the Earth, in 1962. He went back into space in 1998 onboard the shuttle Discovery, making him the oldest person (aged 77) to fly in space.

Action Stations

It's a long, long, way to the stars: if you were at the wheel of the fastest racing car there is, and if it could drive to the stars, how long do you think it would take to get there? A year? A century? How about 4 million years! That's just to the nearest star – most of the ones you can see are much farther away.

LIFE IN SPACE

The International Space Station (ISS), currently being built 350 km above the Earth by 16 nations, will be the size of a football pitch when it is finished.

Three to four times a year, the unmanned Progress robot vehicle docks with the ISS to deliver food, water and fuel, and take away the trash. It burns up as it re-enters Earth's atmosphere – true waste disposal!

Flying High

UNMANNED
SUPPLY VEHICLE

LIVING
QUARTERS

RADIATORS COOL
ISS WHEN IN LINE
WITH SUN

SOLAR
ARRAYS
PROVIDE
POWER

MECHANICAL ARM
FOR ASSEMBLY OF ISS
SECTIONS

DOCKING FOR
SHUTTLES

HE WAS HERE!

Extra parts of the ISS are added by astronauts. David Wolf, held in place by a foot restraint on the Canadarm, is attaching a camera to one of the trusses.

The ISS is the largest man-made satellite orbiting the Earth.

However, that doesn't mean people will never reach them. The plans for the first starship have already been made: a spaceship the size of a city, that will fly for a hundred years. In the meantime, astronauts can live in space for months at a time, on the International Space Station (ISS) that is being constructed in space over years and years.

What's this? Believe it or not, it's a photo of London at night, taken from the ISS. The wiggly line around the bottom edge is the M25, and the dark patches just below and left of the central bright section are Hyde Park and Regents Park.

...ISS

IN THE KNOW...

* Width: approx. 100 m
* Length: approx. 75 m
* Mass when finished: about 450,000 kg
* First launch: 20 November 1998
* Number of orbits per day: 15.7
* Travelling speed: 27,700 km/h

In a Spin

Two spiders called Arabella and Anita were kept on the *Skylab* space station to study the effect of weightlessness on their ability to spin webs. It obviously took its toll, as the spiders spun uneven webs that weren't as strong as the ones they spun before take off.

Ripley's Believe It or Not!®

NO SPACE LIKE HOME

Prior to the ISS, both the USA and Russia had working space stations orbiting the Earth. Skylab (USA) in the 1970s had three crew visits, while Russia's Salyut (1971–82) led to the more successful Mir space station.

In 1869 the first story was published about a space station – made of bricks! It was *The Brick Moon* by Edward Everett Hale.

The longest spaceflight was by the Russian cosmonaut Valeriy Polyakov, who stayed on space station *Mir* for 437 days.

Sections of the ISS are taken into space on board the shuttles *Endeavor*, *Atlantis* and *Discovery* and the Russian crafts *Proton* and *Soyuz*. The first stages were joined together in orbit in 1998.

THAT'S IT!

LONG SHOT

In 2006, a golf ball hit by cosmonaut Mikhail Tyurin entered Earth's orbit. It may still be travelling around the Earth even now! If not, it will fall towards Earth and burn up when it enters the atmosphere. It was hit off the ISS from a special tee attached to a platform, and will probably cover a distance of a billion miles. Now THAT'S a long shot!

Stephen Michalak said he found a UFO at Falcon Lake, Manitoba, Canada, in 1967. As he got closer he appeared to have been burned with a pattern of dots on his chest.

Aliens are Coming!

REALLY?

Several specially designed radio messages have been sent out into space, in the hope that someone will answer. So why haven't they? Well, perhaps they have – in 1977 a radio signal was received that no one has been able to explain in any other way – it was so surprising that the scientist who received it wrote 'Wow!' on the printout.

Do aliens exist? If so, they might have heard from us by now – radio and TV signals that were broadcast 50 years ago, and are travelling out from the Earth at 299,792,458 m/second, have already reached more than 130 stars. Roughly 10% of those stars are likely to have planets – maybe inhabited ones.

EXTRA TERRESTRIALS
Launched in 2009 from Cape Canaveral in Florida, the Kepler telescope is on the lookout for planets in other systems. It will spend at least 3-5 years staring at 100,000 stars in a section of the Milky Way. It's hoped that it will confirm the existence of planets like Earth that are capable of sustaining life.

WOW!

UFO crash victim'

Signs of life

Two Italian professors have found signs of life from outer space! These micro-organisms were discovered concealed inside meteorites, and when put under lab conditions, they began to move and reproduce. Can it be the proof needed for those who believe life exists elsewhere in the Universe?

TALK TIME

In 1967, a ticking radio signal from space was detected. The project to explain it was called 'LGM' for 'Little Green Men'. The source turned out to be a type of spinning star called a pulsar.

Some scientists think that there may be thousands of intelligent civilisations in our galaxy.

In 1960, radio messages were sent to two nearby stars in the hope that intelligent aliens might reply.

More than 30 planets have so far been found in orbit around other stars.

Chatting to aliens on a planet going around another star would need a lot of patience. The nearest such planet goes around a star called Epsilon Eridani, and to send a message there and get a reply back would take 21 years.

twist it!

Alien found in Israel!

This weird 12-cm-long 'alien' was discovered in northern Israel in 1998. Clearly visible are a head, legs, arms and fingers – but could it really be an alien being from another world?

erghh!

Claims that this photograph show an alien recovered from a crashed UFO have been put under scrutiny. The crash was said to have taken place in New Mexico in 1950. The picture was sent to Germany for examination and it is believed to be a hoax.

CODED MESSAGE

The two Voyager spacecraft, both on their way to the stars, are carrying golden discs containing messages for any aliens that might encounter them.

The Voyager and Pioneer space probes should eventually reach other stars, after journeys lasting more than 80,000 years. Plenty of time for them to bump into other beings along the way!

Video recording shows as waves

Image of record being played

Direction of scan needed to play disc

Diagram of hydrogen atom

Location of our sun

Space index

Acknowledgements

COVER (l) © dieter Spears – istockphoto.com, (r) Geoffrey Robinson/Rex Features; **2** Courtesy NASA; **3** (l) © Iuliia Kovalova – fotolia. com, (t/c) Courtesy NASA, (b/c) © Darren Hester – fotolia.com; **4** (c) © Dieter Spears – istockphoto.com; **5** (c) Geoffrey Robinson/Rex Features; **6** (sp) R. Williams (STScI) the Hubble Deep Field Team and NASA; **7** (l) Reuters/Mike Blake, (t/l, t/r, c/l c/r) Rex Features; **8** (t) Courtesy NASA, (b/l) © mario beauregard – fotolia.com, (b/r) Reuters/Ho New; **9** (l) Courtesy of David Hanson, (c) STR/AP/PA Photos, (r) © treenabeena – fotolia.com; **10–11** (c) © suzannmeer – fotolia.com; **10** (l) © icholakov – fotolia.com, (b/l, t/r) Geoeye; **11** (t/l, c, b/r) Geoeye, (t/r) Lewis Whyld/PA Archive/PA Photos; **12** (sp) ESA, (b/r) © suzannmeer – fotolia.com; **13** (c) Courtesy of Yohkoh Project ISAS/Lockheed–Martin Solar and Astrophysics Laboratory/National Astronomical Observatory of Japan/University of Tokyo/NASA, (b/r) © Ekaterina Starshaya – fotolia.com; **14** (sp, b/l) Courtesy NASA; **15** (c/l) Courtesy NASA, (b/r) Courtesy NASA/JPL–Caltech/Galileo Project, (t/l, t/r, t/b/l, c, t/b/r) Courtesy NASA; **16** NASA/Johns Hopkins University Applied Physics Laboratory/Carnegie Institution of Washington; **17** (l) Courtesy NASA, (c) Riedrich Saurer/Science Photo Library, (r) Courtesy NASA; **18–19** (sp) Detlev Van Ravenswaay/Science Photo Library; **18** (t/l) NASA; Greg Shirah, SVS, (b/r) Courtesy NASA; **19** (t) NASA/JPL, (r) NASA/JPL–Solar System Visualization Team; **20** (l) A. Simon-Miller/GSFC/NASA/ESA/STScI/Science Photo Library, (r) Copyright Calvin J. Hamilton; **21** (sp) NASA/JPL/Space Science Institute, (r) David Ducros/Science Photo Library; **22** (t) NASA/ESA/L. Sromovsky, U. WISC/STScI/Science Photo Library, (b) Courtesy NASA; **23** (sp) Chris Butler/Science Photo Library, (b/r) NASA/Kim Shiflett; **24** (l) © Jess Wiberg – istockphoto.com, (r) © Iuliia Kovalova – fotolia.com; **25** (l) © Dennis di Cicco/Corbis, (r) AFP Photo/NASA; **26** (l) © Dragos Constantin – fotolia.com (c, t) ESA; **27** (l) © Bettmann/Corbis, (r) Courtesy NASA; **28** NASA, ESA and A. Schaller (for STScI); **29** (t) NASA/JPL–Caltech/T. Megeath (Harvard-Smithsonian CfA); **30** (sp) X-ray: NASA/CXC/CfA/R.Kraft et al.; Submillimeter: MPIfR/ESO/APEX/A.Weiss et al; Optical: ESO/WFI, (b/l) NASA/JPL–Caltech/B. Brandl (Cornell & University of Leiden), (b/r) NASA/JPL–Caltech/A. Noriega-Crespo (SSC/Caltech), Digital Sky Survey (b/l, b/r) Courtesy of SOHO/[instrument] consortium. SOHO is a project of international cooperation between ESA and NASA; **31** (t/l) NASA, NOAO, ESA, Hubble Heritage Team, M. Meixner (STScI) and T.A Rector (NRAO), (r) NASA, ESA, HEIC and The Hubble Heritage Team (STScI/AURA), (b, l–r) Matt Bobrowsky (CTA INCORPORATED) and NASA, NASA/JPL–Caltech, The Hubble Heritage Team (STScI/AURA/NASA), H. Bond (STScI), R. Ciardullo (PSU), WFPC2, HST, NASA; **32–33** (sp) Mark Garlick/Science Photo Library; **33** (l) Allan Morton/Dennis Milon/Science Photo Library; **34–35** (dp) NASA/JPL-Caltech/L. Allen (Harvard-Smithsonian CfA), (b) Jean-Charles Cuillandre (CFHT), Hawaiian Starlight, CFHT; **34** (t/l) NASA/JPL–Caltech/P. Morris (NASA Herschel Science Center), (b/l) NASA/JPL–Caltech/J. Rho (SSC/Caltech); **35** (l) NASA/STScI, (r) © Jonathan Larsen – fotolia.com; **36–37** (dp) Courtesy NASA; **37** (l) Courtesy NASA, (r) Rex Features, (b) ESA – S. Corvaja; **38** (sp) © Scott Andrews/Science Faction/Corbis, (l, t, r) Courtesy NASA; **39** (l) Courtesy NASA/Carla Thomas, (t) Courtesy NASA; **40** (l, r) Courtesy NASA; **41** (t/c, t/l, c/l, t/r, b/r, l) Courtesy NASA; **42–43** (sp) Courtesy NASA; **42** (b, t/l) Courtesy NASA; **43** (c) Courtesy NASA, (t/r) Image courtesy of Earth Sciences and Image Analysis Laboratory, NASA Johnson Space Center, ISS Crew, JSC, NASA, (b) © altec5 – fotolia.com; **44** (l) © Snaprender – fotolia.com, (c/l) Mary Evans Picture Library, (c/r) AFP/Getty Images; **45** (t/l) AFP/Getty Images, (l) FPL, (c/l) Courtesy NASA, (c/r) Voyager Project, JPL, NASA, (r) © Darren Hester – fotolia.com

Key: t = top, b = bottom, c = centre, l = left, r = right, sp = single page, dp = double page, bgd = background

Every attempt has been made to acknowledge correctly and contact copyright holders and we apologise
in advance for any unintentional errors or omissions, which will be corrected in future editions.